Phantoms of My Imagination

Julia Rhodes

Copyright © 2018 Julia Rhodes

All rights reserved.

ISBN: 0692166068
ISBN-13: 978-0692166062

DEDICATION

To all of the people who believe a word can hold multitudes.

CONTENTS

Sonnet of Transience	1
Wandering Blood	2
Timeless	3
Tainted Sorrow	4
The Grind	5
Untouchable	6
Captive	7
See No Evil	8
Gateway	9
Villanelle for Divinity	10
Locality	11
Tethered	12
Simplicity	13
Serpents of Perfection	14
Cobalt Song	15
Hear No Evil	16
Circulate	17
Haiku for Dawn	18
Haiku for Dusk	19
To See You	20
Consume Me	21
Speak No Evil	22
Sorrows Unheard	23
Thorns	24
Knights With Funny Socks	25
Untraveled	26
Vehement Villanelle	27
Honeybee Woes	28
Entrapping	29
Like the Evergreen	30
Multitudes	31
Hermit	32
Numbing Nature	33

Cloaking	34
By Pencil	35
Bright Individual	36
Dissipate	37
Abduction	38
Reminiscent Rondeau	39
Wrong About the Light	40
Separated By Myself	41
My Passion Is	42
Burn	43
About the Author	45

SONNET OF TRANSIENCE

Thinking of your morbid grin fills our days
Us, lunging towards a darkness eternal
Foolishly drawn towards the brevity ways
Both fearing and seeking the nocturnal

Oh sweet soil, we are meant for the worms
Stroking our masks with your euphonic call
It's a tender contradiction in terms
Ignoring your brisk breath is our downfall

Floating then sinking, one with the benthos
Pleading for distance, you never comply
Drowning, we steep in merciless pathos
Serenity of a wavering sigh

Pining for darkness, wishing to be kissed
Compliance to your everlasting mist

WANDERING BLOOD

        I wander to consider
                What duration has to offer me
           My passion is the nomadic pull
       To sprint towards a land unknown
      And crave the eyes of philosophy
    To witness life's disparities
Veins seep with the tug of unfamiliar
                To capture all duration has to offer me

TIMELESS

Delightful rush of exuberance
Beams erupt across the face
Hands no longer numerous
Light stands still to end the chase
Frozen contradiction so humorous
Immobile juncture will erase

TAINTED SORROW

I want to climb inside of your breath
And see what I can find
Unhinge the dualities within
Such a wonderful mind

I want to know what happens in the end
Even if its tears
Even if its fears
If its unwilling to bend

I want to discover all of your speculations
Of spent and forthcoming nature
To dine in the bliss of familiar
Entrust in your scheming eyes

THE GRIND

Much he marveled at the sensory street drug.
    Eyes of potholes detoxing, screaming.
        Linear sedatives at each corner
    Envelope passersby as they go.
Overdue for their routine slumber,
    They march through the haze to boost the number.

UNTOUCHABLE

There is a universe of infinite possibilities
    That is waiting for me.
An expanse of multitudes and what ifs
    That I might see.
Realities of magnitudes beyond belief
    That might happen to me.
And of these abounding potentialities
    So little I will see.

CAPTIVE

Enraptured psyche bound by association
Complete heart abdication
Perception confines
Instinct exiled to the sidelines
Voices capture in the attic
Leaving originality static
Thorough infiltration
Norm is now predation
Created are the lines
One that undermines
The unsystematic
And crushes the fanatic

SEE NO EVIL

Oblivious to surrounding proceeding
Mouth makes no pleading
To be free from the set breeding
Of minds full of misleading
Compliant to pervasive reading
Stranded evermore unseeing

GATEWAY

Into the void of fantasy
My mind travels to each night
Cultivating a wondrous mentality
Tales of marvel my thoughts do write

Quelling is the fateful fallacy
Of those who choose to fight
The psyche's limitless majesty
Refusing to marvel in all delight

VILLANELLE FOR DIVINITY

Smirked the sky, the allure has always been.
Privy to the corroding blight, must be
solemn, you wade through the bleakness within.

The aroma of green bees can unpin
the bliss of my skin, observe milady,
smirked the sky, the allure has always been.

Blackened and void, dysphoria of sin
has pervaded, tainting reality.
Solemn, you wade through the bleakness within.

Creation soothes the malleable grin
of those who choose to follow me carefree,
smirked the sky, the allure has always been.

Remain uncovered, refuse to give in
to the tale, spun by the plurality.
Solemn, you wade through the bleakness within.

Ask how such a fiction can be spread thin.
Thank the united buzz of the hive bee,
smirked the sky. The allure has always been,
so, solemn, you wade through the bleakness within.

LOCALITY

You are me, a wandering tree,
    Vagrant I see.

        I am you, a mourning dove,
            Hear my woeful coo.

TETHERED

Twisted world tethering through time
A mystery that could eclipse the sun
Seldom divulged, it remains elusive
But for those who learn to endure in darkness
Enigma may be exposed in the moments when
The tether breaks
And darkness is all there is

SIMPLICITY

Doves don't think about existence,
The weight of taxing tariffs,
Or the fear of heights.

They focus on flying the distance,
Not on controversies of sheriffs
Or what dreams mean during the nights.

To be a dove would be freeing in an instance
Merely simple merits
Soaring through highlights

SERPENTS OF PERFECTION

Consider the looking glass
To reveal secluded truths
Within each body lies dormant
An enigma you wish to see
Reflections reveal this mystery
As you parade it for all to see
Knowing eyes of grandeur will be
Scrutinizing your demeanor
You cunningly adorn the mask
Of what you wish to be
When in the looking glass you see

COBALT SONG

Because I could not sing for the wondrous bluebird,
It did so kindly sing to me.

The flighty delight enticing me,
It's ballad so wholly enchanting me.

Euphonic beak retires as
Cobalt feathers withdraw from me.

I am left to solemn contemplation:
Can mortal devise as devastatingly,
As the wondrous bluebird who did so kindly sing to me?

HEAR NO EVIL

> Shouts of falsity veil your ears
> So pleas of veracity cannot permeate
> Complacent hands make fears disappear
> Assurance of grace they create
> Glued down over the years

CIRCULATE

I feel compelled to tell the world
The marvels of all stories told

Soaring above clouds of fantasy
The reader holds the key

To visualize the abounding possibilities
And strive beyond mortal abilities

These fictions of grandeur compel observers
To share what lies within the covers

HAIKU FOR DAWN

Blazing rays rush down
Over a suspecting town
And time it brings round

HAIKU FOR DUSK

Bewitching nightfall,
Listen to the brisk wind sigh,
Waiting reverie.

TO SEE YOU

Like droplets seeping down my window
A caress of the hair so tender
Like blooming colors as sun emerges
And warm sand upon my feet
Like daisies etched upon my skin
Or oozing sweets between my teeth
Like loves immortal breath so sweet
Euphoric bliss eternal

CONSUME ME

I want passion to wrap its hands around me
Squeeze my waist right inside of me
And pull me to the ground

I want passion to rip my hair straight from me
Whisper curses just about me
And hold my head under the ground

I want passion to plague the soul inside of me
Spread its grimace to the face on me
And bury my body below the ground

SPEAK NO EVIL

You see but you do not tell
You hear but you do not discuss
The noble would make a fuss
But you, you choose the spell

A spell of protection from veracity
That hides from those willing
That all truth is chilling
And only the spell is pretty

To notice, you are taught is wicked
Pondering is not promoted
Powers want the truth to be coated
So speak, for you should be livid

SORROWS UNHEARD

Buffalo bills
    Daisy doos
Cockatoo blues

        Barn town shindigs
            Mountain top snow
        Azure eyes burn

Crimson rivers flow
    Flesh like glow.
Blue jay homeruns!

        Freedom sings.
            Children plead.
        Land unknown.

THORNS

Reclusive thistles pierce feeble flesh
Sneaking through the open mesh
Of frail attire in flourishing grasslands
Climbing up to reach the hands
Of wanderers who seek vivid fields
Where they can let down their shields

KNIGHTS WITH FUNNY SOCKS

>Dancing in the ashes
>Dreaming of the moon
>Fire light flashes
>Hoist up the harpoon
>Golden eyelashes
>Back to the pontoon
>Treasure crashes
>All the crew swoon

Group screams "aye aye!"
With riches to buy
All from imagination box
So tighten up the locks
On hordes of mince pie
Or a new hook and eye
Abounding splendor docks
As knights in funny socks
Prance in with their plunder
As pirates of wonder

UNTRAVELED

> A woodland path so rarely traveled
> Holds secrets equally perceived.
> Arms of timber curve down to preserve
> Mysteries of the passage unseen.

VEHEMENT VILLANELLE

Talons of rapture cordially scarring
Grips of ardor mimic impressions be
Never they knew a sound so enchanting

Zealous cries call for the will of granting
Tears of exuberance they all may see
Talons of rapture cordially scarring

Rapidity creates wistful lightning
Delirious, deleterious plea
Never they knew a sound so enchanting

Cherished conjunction forever linking
Dance of yearning makes a silent decree
Talons of rapture cordially scarring

Silent caress leaves moment unthinking
Residual memorandum beastly
Never they knew a sound so enchanting

Parting to a tolerable cooing
Revolving cycle of endless esprit
Talons of rapture cordially scarring
Never they knew a sound so enchanting

HONEYBEE WOES

Woe is me, the peaceful honeybee
Fields of yellow and green
Flowing just for me

>As I return to see my queen,
>In stomp the created,
>Woe is me, the peaceful honeybee.
>
>Fields I no longer see
>The titans, already they flee
>
>Thus drops the peaceful honeybee,
>Woe is no longer me

ENTRAPPING

Deep into that darkness tapping,
All my soul within me unwrapping.
I had dreamt of discriminations trapping,
As of someone spitefully napping.
Echoes despotism, "Mind the gapping!"

And so it came shrilly buzzing,
Deep into that darkness snapping.

The silent suffocation squeezing;
It's eyes wandering, it was pondering.

Mind strays to contradictions.
The impositions bring such sorrow.

Soon my soul grew vagrant,
Deep into that darkness yapping.

Ah, distinctly I was pining.
My contraries I could not awaken.
Eagerly I looked for domination.
I, a disparity, and you an absolute,
Rhapsodizing the infinitude of darkness.

LIKE THE EVERGREEN

I am akin to the noble evergreen.
I rest, soul soaring above,
a seemingly meager piece of nature's facade.

My roots a vital labor of love.
Sheath forever flawed.
Collapse is uncharacteristic of
My spirit unseen.

MULTITUDES

>Mortals enclose delicate multitudes
>Inside every imagination thrives
>Endless possibilities of altitudes
>And boundless internal drives
>To imagine a place where totality strives

HERMIT

Visionary wanderer
Hoarder of reflections
The perceptive hermit holds a key
To understand infinity

Astute conjuror
Of distinct inflections
Lone mind worth the force of a banshee
Discount the crowds who disagree

NUMBING NATURE

Wolves of wonder wandering when
Tremendous tress time treacherous trims
Dangerous dirt drives downward still
As shocking skies send spikes sinking in
Laboring lakes house lugubrious stains
And anguished animals always accommodate

CLOAKING

Graceful abandonment of nature occurs
As they walk out to go passing hers
Adorning of veils each dawn
No longer showing withdrawn
A daily phenomenon

BY PENCIL

Unlimited power to create
Whatever the soul can dictate
Trees of crimson wings
Or skies of ruthless gaze
Worlds of tears with barren kings
Even endless roadways
Potential to control all fate
Just open up the floodgate

BRIGHT INDIVIDUAL

A flick of the wrist, sparks ignites
Match quivers at our sites
Ropes binding down
As I prepare to sin in this ghost town
Another flick, the wood burns bright
Illuminating the tranquil night
The flames stroll closer to your skin
Revenge for the original sin
The wood cracks, sparks fly
I look into your eye
Crimson overtakes the darkness
Maybe this is heartless
The night shines with a melting glow
Like that of the sun as it fades low
As I watch the flames dance upon your skin
I can't help but think
You are a very bright individual

DISSIPATE

Passion engaging
Intrinsic storms raging
Seclusion craving
All experiences fading
Invader cunning
All ardor cutting
Soul thumping
With desire fading

ABDUCTION

Flow of burn kindles exuberance
Delicious waves of toxicity
Unsavory residual blaze
Smoldering mind
Igniting heart
Another to ease the strain

REMINISCENT RONDEAU

Remember me in skies of storm
Or when surrounded by the swarm
Thoughts of me may illuminate
In times of fear and massive weight
I won't demand that you conform

Your image will never deform
Even under unyielding warm
I only hope that in your fate
Remember me…

Even when it seems out of norm
Feel no need to ever perform
A promise to ever captivate
I'll love at an alarming rate
And all I ask is that your form
Remember me…

WRONG ABOUT THE LIGHT

Elusive in nature
It slips through your grasp
But it is not mischievous, you see
It fluctuations in existence
To brighten its experience
For you to cherish
It's subtle presence
A beacon that rotates
Will not always illuminate
So when it comes round
Grasp what rays you can

SEPARATED BY MYSELF

Perpetual introspection
Molds fallacies that do not exist
A ruthless dissection
Of thoughts that cannot be dismissed

MY PASSION IS

A thought that torments my dreams.
In waking hours,
Sat in the periphery,
It taunts.

If I could fly away,
Only to never return
The question would haunt no more.

But earth bound I am.
Wingless, stuck
To ponder what my passion will be.

BURN

Dancing in the ashes
Of bridges burned
And apologies left unsaid
Do not look back
At what is gone
Or those who do not care to leap
Peer ahead and revel in current being
Cross over to the opposing shore
In a fire born shower of promise

RHODES

ABOUT THE AUTHOR

This is Julia's debut book. She enjoys writing poetry in her free time and decided to put those poems together in this collection. She is a college student in Reno, NV, studying English Literature and Psychology. She strives to one day work in the publishing industry; she published this book as her first step into the field of writing.

www.ingramcontent.com/pod-product-compliance
Lightning Source LLC
Chambersburg PA
CBHW061300040426
42444CB00010B/2446